JAGUAR MkII

JAGUAR MkII
Duncan Wherrett

OSPREY
AUTOMOTIVE

Acknowledgements

The Author wishes to thank the individuals and companies listed below for their help and co- operation in connection with the photographs on the following pages:

1, 64, 65. Derek Madgewick, Colin Barnes
2, 54, 55, 76, 77. Peter Hammond
5, 28, 29. Andrew Elliott
8, 9, 11, 12, 14, 15, 16, 17. David Barnes
22, 23, 25, 26, 27. Roy Ridsdale
31, 32, 33, 35. David Bower
36, 37, 38, 39. Harold Mayer
40, 41, 42, 43. Tony Springate
44, 45, 46, 47. Tony Dance
48, 50, 51. Dan Lowe
52, 53. Carriages Vehicle Agency, Oldbury
56, 57, 118, 119. John Brooks
58, 59, 60, 61, 117, 120, 121. Ron Andrews
62, 63. Hurst Park Automobiles, E Molesey

66, 67, 68, 69, 70. Jim Matthews
71. A Swinglehurst
72, 73, 74. Eric Williams
78, 79, 80, 81. Les Ely
88, 89. John Dalton
95. David Binns
96, 104, 109, 114. Three Point Four Ltd.
98, 99. Tom Birch
100, 101, 111, 128. Autocats Ltd, Rayleigh
102, 122. Vicarage Car Co, Bridgenorth
107, 110. Woodlift Joinery Ltd, London
112, 115. Forward Engineering Co, Meriden
116. Country Classic Cars
123. David Manners Ltd, Oldbury

Models and production years

Mark 1 2.4 1955–59
Mark 1 3.4 1957–59
Mark 2 2.4 1959–67
Mark 2 3.4 1959–67
Mark 2 3.8 1959–67
240 1967–69
340 1967–69

Published in 1990 by Osprey Publishing Limited
59 Grosvenor Street
London W1X 9DA

© Duncan Wherrett

British Library Cataloguing in Publication Data

Wherrett, Duncan
    Jaguar Mk. 2
    1. Cars, history
    1. Title
    629.22209

ISBN 1-85532-101-7

Printed in Hong Kong
Page design Paul Kime

Front cover
The unmistakable Mk II Jaguar front end

Rear cover
Spectacular sight: a racing MkII careering through the bend, just like they used to. . .

Half-title page
Cruising Cat. Action shot of a MkII Jaguar taken from the window of a MkII Daimler

Title page
When introduced in 1955, the MkII was available in either Standard trim or, for an extra £21, with 'Special Equipment'. Naturally, the more expensive version featured the characteristic bonnet mascot

Contents

CHAPTER ONE
Sir William and the MkI 6

CHAPTER TWO
The glory years 20

CHAPTER THREE
Restored and restoring 94

Sir William and the MkI

The origins of the Jaguar MkII go back to the early 1950s and the birth of the MkI. Sir William Lyons, the company's head, realised that there was an important gap in the Jaguar range. He saw that while the two seater XK and the opulent MkVII were excellent cars, they were not the cars that a large number of potential Jaguar customers wanted. There was a demand for a smaller, sporting saloon which could carry four or five people in comfort without sacrificing performance or economy.

Being an astute businessman, Sir William also saw that he could reduce manufacturing costs on his other models if he had a high volume product that used components common to the rest of the Jaguar range.

The 2.4-litre saloon that resulted, broke new ground for the company with its monocoque construction, new suspension and engine configuration.

Originally, it had been intended to fit a 2-litre, four-cylinder version of the XK power unit but it was felt that the smoother running characteristics of a six-cylinder engine were better suited to the market niche the car was aimed at. A power unit of this type would also be more acceptable to the North American market which was an important consideration in the company's strategic plans.

The engine that was eventually decided upon was the 3.4-litre, six cylinder XK unit. The capacity was reduced for the new saloon by shortening the stroke.

Jaguar's new engine produced 112 bhp at 5,750 rpm and could return 28 mpg in the compact bodyshell it powered. The 2.4-litre engine was some 3 in. shorter than the 3.4-litre version and many of the parts were interchangeable between the two, including the cylinder head.

The reduction in stroke length and the fact that the bearings were designed for a larger engine meant that the 2.4 litre unit was very strong.

It was mated to a standard Moss gearbox with synchromesh on second, third and fourth gears. A Laycock de Normanville overdrive which operated on fourth gear, was available as an optional extra.

A very early sales brochure, announcing the 2.4-litre MkI

Brilliant newcomer to a distinguished range . . .

THE NEW 2·4 LITRE JAGUAR

SPECIAL EQUIPMENT MODEL
Identified by its handsome Jaguar radiator mascot, the Special Equipment model will make instant appeal to the motorist demanding the utmost in specification and appointments.

TO the already famous range of Jaguars exemplified by the Mark VII and XK140 models, comes the 2·4 litre Jaguar saloon, a brilliant newcomer in which will be found the embodiment of all the highly specialized technical knowledge and engineering achievement that have gained for the name of Jaguar the highest international repute. For over four years Jaguar engineers and technicians have worked to produce, not simply a new model, but an entirely new car of such outstanding merit as to be worthy of presentation to a world which has for long been accustomed to expect great things from Jaguar. How well they have succeeded is made manifest by the specification and performance of the 2·4 litre, a car which derives its character and breeding from every reward of Jaguar endeavour, every phase of Jaguar achievement and every lesson learned in the hard school of international racing. In its outward appearance, the unmistakable Jaguar line of grace is seen with lesser, more compact overall dimensions than those of the Mark VII, yet the interior has been so skilfully planned that full accommodation for five persons is provided and further provision made for generous luggage accommodation. To those motorists whose desire for a car of compact dimensions is a matter of personal preference the opportunity is at last presented, not only for satisfying that desire, but for gratifying a natural wish to own a car the mere possession of which indicates insistence on owning nothing but the best . . . a Jaguar.

As its name implies, the 'Two-point-Four' is powered by an engine of 2·4 litres capacity and is the latest development of the famous six-cylinder, double overhead camshaft, twin carburetter XK engine which, in engineering circles throughout the world, is acclaimed as the most advanced high efficiency production engine in existence. With a power output of 112 brake horsepower and a power/weight ratio of 90 brake horsepower per ton, phenomenal acceleration is placed at the driver's command and, if desired, a maximum speed of over 100 m.p.h. reached with the ease, silence and refinement which are amongst the inimitable characteristics of every Jaguar. Allied to these characteristics are superb road-holding and braking qualities inseparable from all Jaguar cars.

FRONT SUSPENSION SYSTEM
Contributing to the superb riding and roadholding qualities of the 2·4-litre is the front suspension system which incorporates semi-trailing wishbones and coil springs in conjunction with telescopic shock absorbers.

STANDARD MODEL
The standard model, although fully equipped and carrying the same mechanical specification as the Special Equipment model, does not carry various items which many owners prefer either to dispense with or to add later according to their personal preferences.

Early 2.4-litre MkIs had a narrow radiator grille, similar to that used on the XK

This contributed greatly to the car's economy and refinement at speed.

The front suspension of the MkI was unlike anything seen on a Jaguar saloon before. It consisted of a separate front subframe, made from pressed steel, which had two unequal length wishbones attached to it. These sloped backwards and carried the coil springs, shock absorbers and stub axle carriers. The whole front suspension assembly was attached to the body underframe at four points using Metalastic blocks. This helped to prevent road shocks and vibrations being transmitted to the occupants.

There was the drawback, of course, that the front sub-frame had to be dropped down if the sump was to be removed with the engine *in situ*.

The rear suspension was quite unusual. Five leaf springs were used which were fitted up-side-down. The rear ends of the springs were attached to the axle via rubber bonded bushes and the springs themselves were encased in a specially designed block of rubber. The front ends of the springs were mounted on simple rubber pads. Two forward facing torque arms were attached to the axle and these reacted on a crossmember which ran across the back of the rear seat

area. A Panhard rod provided side location for the live rear axle and the same Girling shock absorbers were used as at the front.

One feature which caused comment at the time was the fact that the rear track was narrower than the front. This was apparently dictated by the car's styling more than any technical requirements.

Sir William Lyons takes much of the credit for the car's appearance which was both distinctive and modern.

The interior was sumptuously fitted out with deep pile carpets, leather upholstery and lavish amounts of walnut veneer.

The 2.4-litre saloon was released to the public in October 1955 with manual transmission only. It was available in either Standard trim or as a Special Equipment version. The 'Special Equipment' included a rev-counter, twin Lucas fog lamps, a bonnet mascot, a heater and courtesy lights. Not surprisingly most buyers opted for the Special Equipment 2.4 as it only cost a further £21. In fact, very few Standard models were sold and they are exceptionally rare today.

The MkI was an instant success and the motoring press of the time hailed it as "one of the most exciting small saloons around."

Left

One of the most unusual features of the MkI was the difference in track between the front and rear wheels. This was concealed, to some extent, by the full spats that were fitted

Above

Despite its small size, the rear light cluster on the MkI still incorporates the rear light, the brake light and the indicator

Above
The MkI featured a rather neat interior light design

Right
As with the other models, the engine bay is dominated by the air filter

Above
*Sir William Lyons, being a non-smoker, did not think it was necessary to fit an
ashtray to the MkI. Under pressure from his design team he relented. The ashtray
is there, hidden behind a wood fillet, underneath the dashboard, just below the
ignition switch*

Right
*The 2.4-litre MkI was produced between 1955 and 1959. This particular example
is virtually standard and has under 25,000 miles on the clock*

Above
A MkI is a rare sight on the race track. This one is being driven by Brian Stevens

Right
There are a number of different schools of thought when it comes to restoring Jaguar MkIs

CHAPTER TWO
The glory years

While the MkI was a successful and popular car – nothing lasts forever. Criticisms had been levelled at the handling and the car's appearance, The thickness of the window and door pillars particularly had been described as 'clumsy'. The men from Browns Lane, Coventry where the cars were built, recognised that the basic product was sound but that it needed to be updated if it were to continue its previous spectacular sales.

The results of their labours was the MkII. While most of the original dimensions remained the same the new car had a fresher, lighter look about it. This was achieved by significantly increasing the glass area, beginning with a deeper windscreen, matched by deeper, wider side windows.

The doors were substantially altered to eliminate the thick window surrounds that had attracted such criticism. The full door frames were also dropped. Instead, on the new model, the doors terminated at waist level and chromium window frames were bolted to the door sections. This method of construction followed American practice.

Few changes were immediately obvious at the front of the car, though some had been made. The foglights were placed where the dummy horn grilles had been on the MkI. The side lights were moved to a position on top of the wings and the radiator grille was revised as well. The new version had a thicker central rib in addition to the row of thin slats.

The interior of the car was totally new. For the first time in any production Jaguar the main instruments were placed directly in front of the driver.

Under the bonnet the MkII used a range of three engines; the 2.4-litre, the 3.4-litre and the 3.8-litre. The 2.4 engine was basically the same as that used in the MkI but the power output was raised

Surprisingly, even though the Jaguar MkII is a fast appreciating classic, this particular example fetched just £2,500 when sold at auction in May 1989

from 112 bhp to 120 bhp. This was achieved by fitting the B-type cylinder head. An increase in all up weight, however, meant that performance was down on that of the 2.4-litre engined MkI.

It is said that Jaguar's public relations managers were careful not to lend journalists 2.4-litre MkIIs because they could not quite manage 100 mph and this might have seemed rather a let down.

Fuel consumption was fairly similar to the larger engined models so motorists tended to prefer these.

The 3.4-litre MkII used a revised 3,442 cc engine that had been developed for the 1957 model year XK150s and MkVIIIs. This incorporated larger diameter exhaust valves, high lift camshafts and new porting.

This engine was rated at 210 bhp and gave the car a top speed close to 120 mph. It was somewhat slower on acceleration than the MkI, again because of additional weight.

Below, right and overleaf
Roy Ridsdale is an enthusiast of the old school. While the current trend is to buy classic cars as an investment rather than as an expression of enthusiasm, he carries out all his own maintenance and still uses his 3.4-litre MkII regularly

The 3.8-litre MkII, on the other hand, had no equal in the saloon car world when it came to top speed and acceleration.

Even cars such as the Aston Martin DB4 could only just match its 0–60 mph times. If price became a factor in the equation then there was no contest at all. In October 1959 the Aston Martin DB4 retailed for £3,755; the 3.8-litre MkII £1,779.

The enlarged capacity was achieved by increasing the diameters of the cylinders bores from 83 mm to 87 mm. This had been done before by private owners but tended to result in cracks appearing between the cylinders. Jaguar overcame this problem by redesigning the block and inserting dry liners.

The MkII's suspension was very similar to the MkI's. The same leaf spring and separate front cross member assembly was used.

Experience had proved drum brakes were inadequate for a car as heavy and powerful as the 3.4-litre MkI. Consequently, all MkIIs were fitted with servo-assisted disc brakes.

Like all its major components the MkII's bodyshell owed much to the MkI. Indeed, virtually all the non-exterior pressings were shared with the earlier car.

It says much for Sir William Lyons' vision that the MkII remained substantially unaltered throughout its production life. The only major variant being a Daimler badged model which featured a V8 engine.

This came about after Jaguar Cars Limited bought Daimler in May 1960. The acquisition gave Jaguar access to an excellent V8 engine which was promptly fitted into a MkII shell. The results of this experiment were very encouraging. So much so that after detail changes to accommodate the new power unit and certain badge engineering, the Daimler derivative was put into production.

It was never planned that the Daimler should replace any of the MkII models. The intention was that it should develop a market position of its own which it duly did.

In many ways it was a better car than the 2.4-litre MkII. The engine was lighter and this improved the handling and reduced the effort required to manoeuvre the car. However the Daimler brand name commanded a different customer loyalty and production was terminated after a total of 8,880 cars had been made.

Further proof that Roy Ridsdale is a Jaguar enthusiast who prefers to drive his pride and joy rather than polish it

When Andrew Elliott bought this 1961, 2.4 it was in desperate need of restoration. He brought it up to concours standard himself, renewing the cross-members, the sills, the door frames and many of the panels in the process. In addition, he resprayed the car its current Old English White and did much of the work on the upholstery and woodwork

Right and following pages
A 1966 3.8 fitted with a manual overdrive and finished in British Racing Green. The sun-roof is non-standard

Above
The large air filter seems to dominate the engine

Left, above and overleaf
Harold Mayer bought his 2.4-litre MkII new in 1964. He has maintained it so well that, over the years, it has won more than 50 concours awards. The air filter used on the 2.4 was different from that used on other models

In its day, very little could match the MkII's speed and acceleration. Possibly this is the reason why parking a MkII outside a bank tended to arouse suspicion

Left
Despite its aerodynamic appearance the MkII has a rather poor drag coefficient

Above
The spare wheel fits neatly into the boot and the comprehensive toolkit fits neatly into the centre of the spare wheel

Above
The factory-fitted disc wheels

Right
Leather trim was fitted as standard

Left
The MkII was a favourite with the ladies' man

Above and overleaf
This Series I E-type makes a perfect partner for the MkII

A classic Jaguar car can make a novel form of wedding transport

The very neat and practical sun-roof

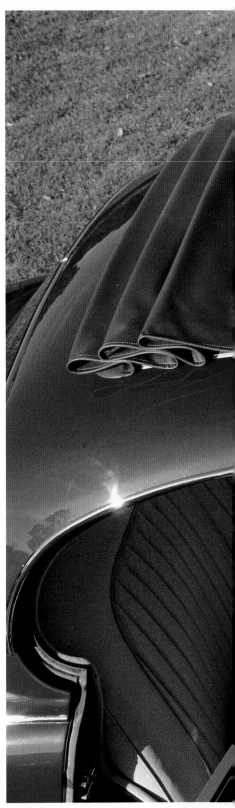

Above
One of the four interior lights

Opposite above
A well finished door catch

Opposite below
The leather trim on the doors added to the air of luxury

Opposite above
Interestingly, the handbrake is mounted to the door side of the driver in right-hand drive cars

Opposite below
The rear quarter-light has changed little over the years

Above
The front and rear door handles are slightly different and are frequently confused with one another. This one can be identified as a rear handle due to the angled edge which lines up with the door

Right
The bonnet catch

Above
A charming feature of the MkII was the picnic tables which folded up into the front seats

Right
The engine bay viewed with the massive air filter removed. The battery cover should slope forward to allow any accumulated rain water to drain away when the bonnet is opened

This 3.8-litre model came to light recently, having been stored for over 18 years. It is in excellent condition and has only 4,500 miles on the clock. It has an unusual Opalescent Bronze finish

A MkII seen with its Daimler
stablemate. While the external
differences are quite subtle, the power
units are totally different. The
Daimler's being a V8 designed by
Edward Turner

A 2.5-litre Daimler with the distinctive ribbed radiator grille

Above
The car has to earn its keep towing a caravan to shows

Opposite above and below
The wheels carry their own insignia. Wire wheels have a certain glamour especially when someone else has to clean them!

The Daimler version dispensed with the normal Jaguar console and this allowed bench seats with arm rests to be fitted

A Daimler still in use as everyday transport

In September 1967 the MkII was superseded by the 240 and 340 model Jaguars. Cosmetically these were similar to the cars they replaced barring the use of Ambla cloth upholstery instead of leather, the replacement of the front fog lamps by horn grilles and the fitting of slimline bumpers with matching over-riders. Frequently, leather seats and fog lights are fitted by enthusiasts, leaving the bumpers as the only distinguishing mark

Left
What better way to spend a Sunday morning?

Above
Occasionally rare cars like this 340 can be found lying in forgotten corners. A 2.4-litre MkII, with a single figure chassis number, is said to be resting in a scrapyard in the south of England. A Holy Grail for Jaguar enthusiasts?

The car pictured is an extremely rare 340 fitted with a 3.8-litre engine. This type was only available on special customer order. There is some confusion over just how many were produced but the figure certainly does not exceed 11 examples. Of these only this is known to survive. It is finished in Opalescent Maroon

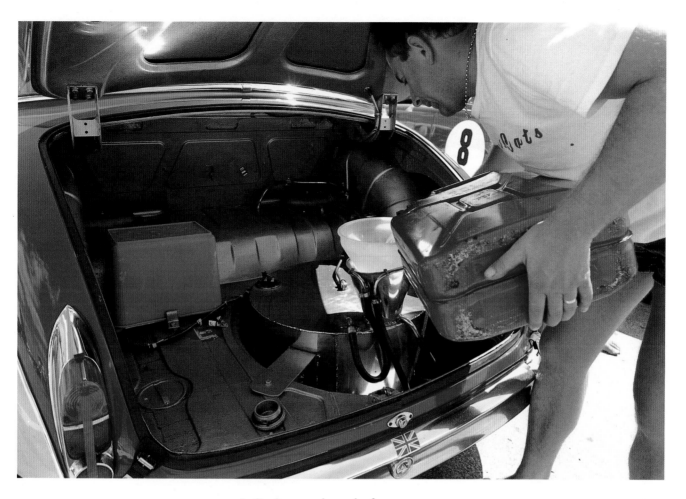

Left, above and overleaf
A few people still turn out with their MkIIs in racing trim but the number is dwindling. Les Ely's red and silver car is arguably one of the smartest

Above
Race prepared MkIIs frequently had their bonnets louvred to improve the flow of
air around the cylinder heads and carburettors

Right
Children and members of the public absentmindedly swinging cameras are an
owner's nightmare at concours events

Inspection time at a concours d'elegance

Jaguars can frequently be seen at owners' club shows up and down the country

Some owners are becoming more and more reluctant to take their increasingly valuable MkIIs onto the roads. This is certainly not the case here. John Dalton has owned his 3.4 since 1978 and uses it daily in and around the streets of London

Above, right and overleaf
In racing trim a Jaguar is a stirring sight. The commonly observed body roll in tight cornering adds to the excitement, but rarely will these beasts go over on their roofs

With prices of original MkII Jaguars being what they are, one wonders whether these race track refugees will eventually receive the full restoration treatment and be advertised in the 'Collectors Cars' columns...

CHAPTER THREE
Restored and restoring

The MkII Jaguar was a remarkable blend of elegance, breathtaking acceleration, good top speed and sheer value for money. It was a car that won the hearts and minds of all those who drove it. Yet, remarkably the MkII simply faded away.

The model name disappeared in 1967 although the bodyshell soldiered on for another 19 months as the 240 and 340.

Various changes were made in the specification to keep these cars competitively priced and maintain sales. The general opinion was that the MkII had gone down market, that it was 'no more than a sportier Ford Zephyr'.

This and old age finished the MkII. While its straight line performance certainly had not dated, its heavy steering, handling and ride were no longer up to the standards expected of a Jaguar.

Its passing left the same gap in the Jaguar range that the MkI had originally been designed to fill. Much to their cost, Jaguar has never filled that gap with a comparable compact, high performance saloon.

In some ways, this is why the MkII is so sought after today. There is nothing of the same quality that has the MkII's charisma and performance.

Prices for MkII Jaguars have soared recently but then this is true of all classic cars. If you are looking for a MkII then there are a few things to bear in mind.

It is better to pay more for a low mileage, one owner car than buy a 'restoration project'. No Jaguar is cheap to restore.

When purchasing any second-hand car, do not be swayed by the fact that it is exactly what you are looking for, be objective and where possible bring someone who is not a Jaguar enthusiast with you.

Attempting a complete restoration in a private garage is a massive undertaking which requires a tolerant family. Dave Binns is about to fit a new wing to this Jaguar 240

A gleaming exterior can hide body filler, structural corrosion and a host of other horrors. Generally the prospective buyer should first check for ill fitting panels. The gaps between doors and other panels should all be relatively even. Examine the bodywork for ripples or unevenness paying particular attention to newly painted areas and freshly undersealed sections.

Specifically, on the MkII the front valance, which runs across the full width of the car just behind the bumper, is very prone to rusting.

Underneath the valance is a crossmember. Due to its position road dirt tends to accumulate on it and again it rusts through very easily. The crow's feet at the ends of the crossmember which support the leading edge of the wings tend to rot as well.

Repair sections are available for these areas and damage in these locations is relatively easy to rectify.

The front wings themselves rust in many places but especially in the region of the side light housing. The indicator housing also suffers as mud tends to collect behind the fittings on the inside of the wing. The extreme edges of the wheel arches act as a mud trap as well.

Paint bubbles around the rear half of the wing tends to indicate severe problems in this area. Water collects up around the edges of the inner closing panels and gets past the rubber sealing strip as it deteriorates. Damage then occurs to both the wing and the inner sill.

The front wing area can prove to be the most expensive to repair but a variety of part panels are available.

The under bonnet areas are relatively free of rust traps but the inner wings at the rear should be checked. A major cause for concern is the bulkhead behind the battery. If the battery has leaked this could be suffering from severe corrosion which will not become apparent until the battery is removed.

In the centre section of the bodywork the most important points are the floor pan and the inner sills. It is necessary to get underneath the car to examine these properly.

The door bottoms are very prone to rust out as the window sealing was never very effective. If this has occurred the door will have to be reskinned.

If possible, when examining a car, remove the rear seats and check the rear shock absorber mountings. The Panhard rod mountings should be thoroughly examined as well.

Cars awaiting restoration

A body in the process of being privately prepared for a respray

It is a sad fact but there are very few areas of the MkII that can be assumed to be sound. Mechanically, however, the Jaguar MkII is strongly built and should be relatively trouble-free. That is said assuming that regular maintenance has not been neglected.

The Metalastic mounting blocks which support the front suspension will perish and split in time and it is vital that these are replaced.

Similarly, the rear leaf spring mounting should be checked as this can collapse, allowing the spring to rest directly on the bodywork.

Gearboxes and back axles are immensely strong and should not cause any problems. Where an overdrive unit is fitted it is important to clean the filters regularly.

Jaguar engines are renowned for their longevity and should easily reach 100,000 miles without major overhaul, provided they have been properly maintained. However, do not think that a car with a sound body and a poor engine is a bargain. Engine rebuilds can cost upwards of four figure sums. Finally, as the Romans used to say, *caveat emptor* – let the buyer beware!

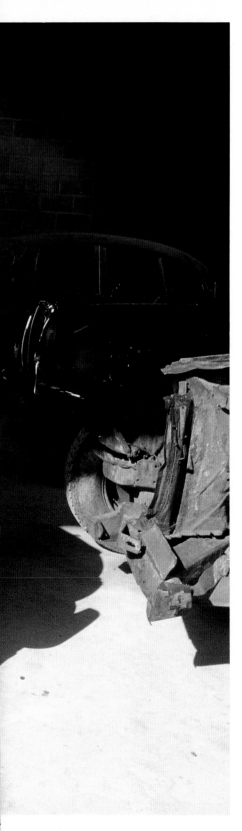

Seen here are a few of the MkIIs awaiting restoration by Autocats. In the foreground is an example of the finished article

Left
The Vicarage Car Company has a steady stream of MkIIs passing through its impressive workshop facility. The company specializes in refurbishing and modernising cars. Customers frequently request the firm to fit electric windows, five-speed gearboxes, air conditioning and more luxurious trim while keeping the exterior standard

Above
Patrick Lacey at work on a restoration project. He carries out high quality rebuilds for the discerning driver

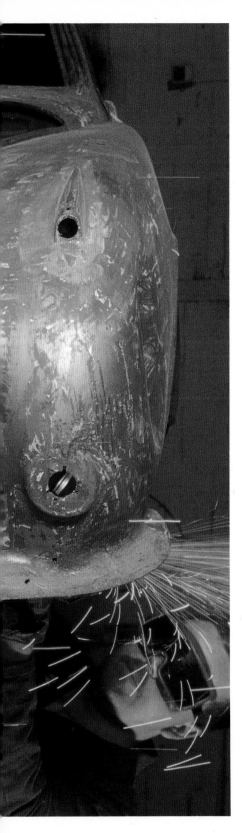

Left
Older MkIIs frequently require major surgery to rectify severe structural corrosion

Above
After new metal has been welded into place and filled in, it has to be carefully sanded down to achieve a perfect finish

Some professional restorers prefer to use two-pack acrylic paints because of their durability. When respraying a car it should be taken back to the bared metal and acid washed. An etch primer should then be applied before the primer proper. Sometimes one of these two stages are omitted. An uneven finish on some cars is due to the preceding layers of paint being badly keyed and flatted

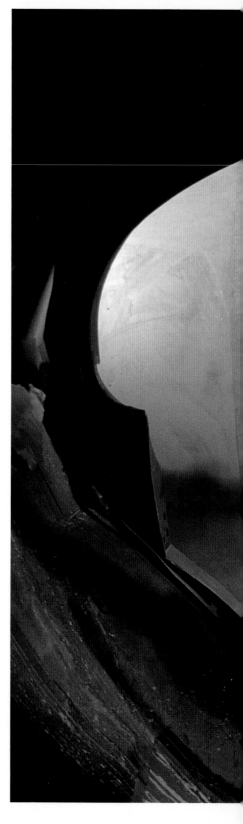

Right
The Three Point Four company specializes in restoring MkIIs to their original specification. It favours using cellulose paint instead of modern 'synthetic' clear overbase

Above
The Jaguar MkII was never offered with either a vinyl roof or two-tone paintwork as a factory option. These modifications are the work of private individuals

Here, the interior trim is being finished

Left
The six cylinder, XK engine was and is one of the main attractions of the MkII

Above
Here all the parts of an XK engine laid out in order. This cuts down the possibility of mistakes when rebuilding the unit

Left
A finished engine being removed from a test bench

Above
Fitting a valve into an XK cylinder head. Cylinder heads were colour coded to aid identification. This is from a 3.8-litre engine

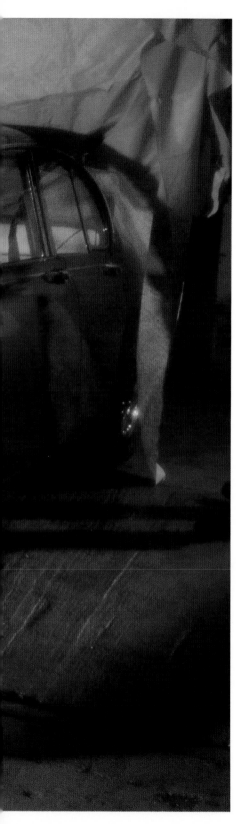

Left

County Classic Cars have produced their own version of the celebrated John Coombs' MkII. It has a 4,542 cc XK engine, mated to a five-speed, Getrag gearbox which transmits the power to the road via a 3.07:1 final drive. This combination gives a claimed 145 mph at 4,420 rpm. The suspension and brakes have been uprated and rack-and-pinion steering has been fitted. An alternator has taken the place of the original dynamo and oil coolers have been installed. While purists may be offended, County Classic Cars decided their MkII also needed electric windows and a remote control CD Player

Above

A worm's eye view of a spotless underside

A great deal of time and money was spent restoring this 3.4-litre MkII to its present concours quality. It is standard throughout with a dark, metallic Opalescent Blue finish

overleaf
A standard 3.8-litre model, beautifully restored by Ron Andrews

Above
Spare parts and new panels for the MkII can still be obtained reasonably easily.
David Manners has a vast quantity of Jaguar spares including the world's largest
stockpile of MkII parts

Left
The MkII looks rather strange as a convertible. It appears rather irreverent to
mutilate a classic car like this, especially as time is taking its toll of surviving
examples anyway. Surely it could not have been worthwhile, to develop a
convertible, considering the limited number of people who will want such a
conversion

Above and overleaf
A good day can produce a pride of Jaguars

The MkII offers the DIY enthusiast 'plenty of scope'